RHYME

REASONS

John Welsh

chipmunkapublishing
the mental health publisher

Published by
Chipmunkapublishing
United Kingdom

http://www.chipmunkapublishing.com

FOREWORD

The following compilations are drawn from book 4 of my manic trilogy!
That statement could set the tone for its place in the annals of daftness.

Choosing 8 linked verses from a vast selection covering the last 10 years and writing an explanation about each compilation allows me I feel to be more random as I was before in my previous book layouts with only alphabetical order of my poems being the pattern.
So it could be a heady mixture of love/lust, escapism, weird or rib cracking comedy.
Read on and find out if the book can be judged by it's foreword or it's cover.
My terminology and phrasing has always been at the least suspect.
Some is I feel easily decipherable like Com-etry (Comedy poetry) but Off-etry and Sketch-etry etc. may take a bit more figuring out.
I have previously stated that I do not read much poetry but I have written shed loads.
I call it life poetry and is often triggered by sights, sounds and even smells.
My bipolar mind often reacts quickly to situations and the usual sleepless nights have writing and toilet breaks.
Recently I have been revisiting some of my archives and I have a few stories that I want to complete and even look to produce into another media form.
So not just bestsellers, Oscars and Grammy's.
WATCH THIS SPACE.

Like some writers I have spoken to, the pandemic slowed and often stopped their output. Mine did but I will include a verse that came out in that terrible time.

i.e. **LOCKDOWN LOCKS (OR COMBING OUT OF COVID)**

In the absence of a stylist
With a closed sign at the barber
I thought I would get creative
Though the problem grew much harder.
My options were increasing
As my headgear did not fit
Sprouting tufts came out all sides
I looked like a hairy git.
I still wanted windswept and interesting
A wide parting with managed sides
But to keep the vision I sometimes had
I bought some large hair slides.
Maybe a top, side or back knot
Could I try a Nordic ponytail or plait
Or Italian slick using the finest oil
Then slide on a hat
A Brazilian comb over could do it
to keep my tresses trim
or even an Elvis.
I could look like him
"Something for the weekend Sir"
Nudge wink the barber said
"no just a jar of Brylcreem
To go onto my head"

John the poet April 2021

Trag-etry

Trag-etry can also be called Lov-etry. It is poetry
about relationships that do not always go well.
I once featured in a local newspaper article titled
"Dumping your lover, do it with my poetry"
I stressed to the journalist that I was not
unromantic just that there should be a kinder way
than text dumping or anti-social posting.
The last two poems in this section fall into the
category of Sketch-etry.
This translates as poetry for two readers.
(MALE/FEMALE)
It can get a bit lonely on an open mic stage so this
was my cure.

John the poet

DID I SAY?

Thoughts are important
But words mean much more
A smile says a lot
And to know what for

Did I say?
Because I thought this
And it's not even a special day
Except maybe it is

If it's fun I am after
I come to you
No looking back
Only forward will do

You were my first thought
Feeling good about today
Text me, call me
Did I say?

John the poet

DIVAESQUE

I know I am being followed
that face in all my fans
the scrutiny, the intensity
unsettling my plans
I want security trebled
It's a stalker I am sure
I know that all do love me
But this attention needs a cure
When I am out and blowing kisses
Or shining on my stage
I sense a watching presence
That's very hard to gauge
No one knows my background
A star that rose from grime
I clawed and fought my way up
To release myself from slime
The press and tv love me
I am like no one, no other
This questioning face always
Reminds me of my mother

John the poet

AURAL SOCKS

Pardon did I hear you right
Are you up for some game's
Now let me warn you here and now
That I know most positions and names
I was once a 69er
But now I'm a 57
I nearly died of suffocation
As I was looking up to heaven
The internet has provided me
With new found skills and motion
So you go get your costume
And I will apply the lotion
Silver sex is slow you know
A game of more than two halves
So start with stimulating the feet
You may never reach the calves
So with dementia and arthritis
The outcome may often fail
But it's like Xmas and all your birthdays
If you reach the hairy grail
All I need is a longer run up
Maybe a pill to pep me up
But what's probably a safer bet
Is sipping tea from the same cup.

John the poet

AN IMPERFECT BEAUTY

Knock me sideways
Speechless or stunned
Can I face you full on
My guts are upturned

Dare I say it out loud
Danger! Danger! Arse!
You know your effect on me
It's living in my face

Two months on I question
The dye, the caps, the creams
Do I really know this woman?
Do I really know my dream's?

John the poet

A RECIPE FOR LIVING

Take a handful of happiness
mortar and pestle it with love
add a pinch of playful humour
whisk with the wings of a peace dove

Truth can be your side dish
Freshly picked that day
Nothing left to dry and age
A taste that will always stay

All the herbs and spices
Cannot disguise the whole
Fish and meat are only complete
When passion is in the bowl.

John the poet

BITTTER AND TWISTTED

This relationship is now over
You took more than you gave
What once was good and honest
Is dead! I will spit upon your grave

I hope the rest of your existence
Has pain, cold and loss
If I hear of all your misfortune
I will fleetingly give a toss

What did I ever see in you
You are an anagram of love gone bad
You take and break then take some more
My testimony to you is SAD

later
Forgive me for that diatribe
That rant, the bile, the hate
Maybe you could consider taking me back
Or is it just too late?

John the poet

ALL AT ONCE I KNEW (PT 1)

We had been so happy
Though it started out as lust
I could not keep my hands off
Your bum, your bits, your bust
But recently I have noticed
Some things not seen before
Your arse is fat, your boobs are small
I don't fancy you anymore
So don't say that I am impulsive
Walk out on just a whim
It's been a twenty year secret
Yes the postman, <u>I fancy him</u> !

pt 2

Am I supposed to act surprised
Your new news isn't new
Iv'e known about your postal vote
since nineteen ninety-two
While you been sorting parcels
Licking stamps and getting franked
Well, my truly late delivered husband
I have been regularly thanked
The butcher and the grocer
Like a girl who is big and proud
And the candlestick maker
Well, he likes a girl who is loud
We could stay together for the cats
And what about dear old mum
Maybe I can dress like a postie
And you can get to like my bum!

John the poet

A GAME OF TWO HALVES WITH NO REF
(Relationship & emotion facilitator)

Female   I miss you in your absence
I miss you when you are here
I missed you with that teapot
That went past your left ear

Male   Darling, we got talking football
And the beer was oh! So sweet
We had to go out to the practice ground
To show off our incredible feet

Female   I remember why I loved him
Yesterday and way back then
He could charm the birds down from the trees
And eggs out of a hen

Male   Oh! Honey, I beseech you
I will grovel on all fours
You don't understand beer and football talk
You say I am late by 24 hours!

Female   Well he's gone and out of my hair
I've changed the locks and dropped the latch
I think I'll call my girlfriends round
Drink some lager, watch the match

Male   I'm back in the pub with my buddies
Though the beer doesn't taste quite as good
I moan we never had much in common
And never talked about where we stood

Both
The moral of this poem
Is to make time for a chat
And find out if your partner
Is interested in this and that

John the poet

I have always maintained that poetry should be spoken words.
The personal content can often be misunderstood and to have the benefit when possible, of the author reading their own work, with pauses and emphases as a bonus then it can bring the meaning to life.
Since Covid the opportunity to do open mic sessions has dwindled but as I write this in September 2022 I sense a growing list of venues

John the performer

COM-ETRY

These poems originated as comedic stories (long jokes) that I have picked up and recited possibly too many times over bar room tables. They are always hilarious after a couple of pints.

 had an idea to recycle them into poetry i.e. com-etry = comedy poetry and I can only hope that when read or even better listened to when performed (as jokes should be) they will seem funny.

Some of these go way back in my life (maybe 30-50 years) and are probably a bit non-pc but I have enjoyed giving them a new lease of life and hope you enjoy the stories told as well as the inevitable punchline.

 apologise now to The Irish, pet lovers and cowboys etc.

Alongside these I developed a genre called Sing-etry which is where I ask my audience to name that tune. These as it is read only are not included in this compilation.

John the poet

A DAY AT THE SEASIDE

Yeah! we are off to the seaside
Our annual summer trip
What fun we will have
Oh yes! we will let rip

Me and my mate Billy
Do everything together
Playing out and playing about
In any kind of weather

As it was a sunny day
We headed for the beach
Our parents said keep in sight
Not too far out of reach

We headed for the sea edge
Racing and chasing down the sand
We decided to have a paddle
That was always planned

Off came plimsoles and socks
Our excitement we could hardly bear
I mentioned my feet were cleaner than his
Yes! he said I didn't come last year!

John the poet

THE INVENTOR OF CAT'S EYES

My inventions come to me in strange ways
And I act on what I see
I try to come up with unique ideas
That may change history
I hope that my new creations
Help and even save lives
And of course when I am a millionaire
I can attract potential wives
One night as I pulled out of my drive
With my headlights shining out
They picked up a nocturnal cat approaching
With bright reflecting eyes no doubt
It was an easy decision to make
So clear like bright as day
Replicate that pussy's eyes
Then fit them in the highway
I often think of fate and timing
Sometimes about angels with a harp
If I had seen that same cat going away
I could have made pencils be sharp

John the poet

PADDY'S CAR

Paddy won the lottery
Be-Jasus he was glad
His friends had always taunted him
His poverty drove him mad

He decided to splash out
And ordered a shiny new car
The latest Datsun sports model
It could go fast and could go far

He would unveil at a party
Invites all went out
He was feeling rather grand
With something to boast about

The week before the party
The car refused to start
So he called in a mechanic
Who said "it needs a part"

Paddy said "WELL GET ONE
I HAVE TO GET IT RIGHT"
So calls and e-mails started flying
Right throughout the night

London, Frankfurt and Beijing
All replied no part in stock
Only the main Datsun plant
Could supply the cog that's crocked

Paddy was going frantic
Telling all to please be quick
The special part was despatched
From Tokyo by fast jet, supersonic

The plane arrived at Heathrow
Just as the weather did turn bad
Paddy saw the weather forecast
Be-Jasus he was mad

But not to be defeated
He hired a private plane
With a derring-do but expensive pilot
To fly through wind and rain

There was thunder and hurricanes
Hailstorm, wind and rain
The pilot thought the worst had passed
When a lightning bolt hit the plane

The gusts and swirls were buffeting
As the plane crossed the Irish shore
The part fell out of the holed fuselage
That used to be a door

Down below in the sodden fields
Murphy and Shamus worked the bogs
The projectile landed close to them
" Look it's raining Datsun cogs"

I AM ALL OF A FLUTTER

A man went to his doctor
And said I think I am a moth
He was prescribed two types of tablets
And told to take one or even both

The man returned after one week
Stating he was no better
The doctor was not surprised
And handed him a letter

It was an appointment with a specialist
Next evening a psychoanalyst second to
none
But the man returned to the doctor's
door
Next night as his light was on

John the poet

DEAD PET

My friend was so upset
Her son's pet hamster had died
He was inconsolable
And both of them had cried

I tried to be positive
And said life's circle would go on
I had read an article about regeneration
On a site called wastenot.com

It said don't bury your loved ones
But turn them into food
You absorb them into your being
And the protein will do you good

So next day in the kitchen
We minced and mixed the pet
The recipe on the website
Said a preserve we would get

Two weeks later came
And I spread it on my loaf
And as I expected
It tasted really gross

I threw it out the window
And washed out the taste
Then made a point of contacting
That site called crap.notwaste.

The following spring was weird
Daffodils flowered all on my lawn
I could not understand it
As bulbs I had not sown

I called my friend who came around
To inspect my garden panoram
She said "yes very strange
It's usually tulips from hamster jam"

John the poet

BIG BLACK JAKE

A lonesome thirsty cowboy
Was staggering down the trail
He had been out west for three days now
His strength was about to fail
He was dreaming about beer and women
But beer most of all
A large foaming mug of froth
Into which he was about to fall
But just as he was giving up
Some buildings came in sight
Mirages usually were more attractive
This place was not too bright
Still! I bet it's got a saloon
With beer and girls and beer
So, he hurried on as best he may
If he could, he would even cheer
The saloon bar was dusty
As dusty as his throat
He croaked out large one bartender
As he stood in a dried-out moat
A few other rednecks
Sat at tables playing poker
But his gaze and thoughts were on his pint
Steady lad he said no choker
Just as he grasped the cool handle
A commotion caused him to frown
A cowboy rushing in exclaimed
BIG BLACK JAKE is coming to town
Every cowboy as one man
Ran quickly out the door
The lonesome thirsty cowboy
Was left shaking on that floor

But no he said I will make a stand
I deserve this beer and more
so, he stood up tall to enjoy his drink
Although he was only five foot four
He felt a small vibration
He saw it in his beer
He moved over to the door
To watch his nemesis appear
Along the street came a buffalo
With horns as wide as barns
And on him rode a man in black
Huge with muscular arms
He looked tough and he looked hard
A sneer below his hat
His mighty beast could walk over cowboys
And leave them squashed flat
This lonesome still thirsty cowboy
Thought a welcome might keep death at bay
"I cannot stop said the booming reply
BIG BLACK JAKE is on his way!"

John the poet

THE AWARD SPEECH

I chose animal husbandry as my subject
And studied long and hard
To know all about the livestock
Found in and around the farmyard
I looked at chickens, goats, and pigs
Horse's sheep and cattle
Keeping animals well and healthy
Is a never- ending battle
My specialist area was dairy herds
And for twenty years now
I have sought to find a cure
For the bowing of back legs of cows
Cows are ruminants you know
Eating grass from dawn till light endures
All that grazing in those fields
Produces plenty of manure
It wasn't the most pleasant of jobs
And praise I seemed to lack
But I thank today all my eminent colleagues
For this first pat on the back

John the poet

A LIONS TAIL

I got a job as a handyman in a local zoo
The owner showed me the jobs that I could do.
First up was in the insect house tending and
cleaning bees.
The fiddly job was long so thinking I was the
bee's knees
I sluiced some water through the hive
Alas I heard no buzzing as no bees were alive
The boss was disappointed at my disclosure
And told me to throw the dead into the big cat
enclosure.
We don't waste anything here he said
And directed me to a new task instead.
The chimps in the monkey house were
naughty and quick
I was to clean their cage and control them with
a stick.
They ganged up on me and I fought them as I
left.
The result was 2 dead, 2 lamed. I was bereft.
Oh! the boss was not impressed but did
forgive my deed
And instructed me to take the apes to be
another lion feed.
Then it was off to the fish tank to clean off all
the scum.
Lots of exotic species back and forward swum
My brush head caught the plug chain located
in the base.
The water ran out quickly, a fishy death race.
"That's it "said the boss when he heard
Employing you I cannot afford.

Here are your cards and wages and your final
act today
Is to toss the dead fish into the big cat bay.

&

2 lions were lying down together
Yawning, stretching, lazing in the good
weather
There's not much to this place, not much to
see
Though the food is great
Fish, chimps, and mushy bees.

John the poet

OFF-ETRY

This translates to escapism in its many forms.
Either going off physically or losing yourself in dreams etc.
It is a thread running through a lot of my work and has been a pattern in my life.
"When the going gets tough, the tough leave by the nearest exit"
My condition lets me take so much stress and emotional upheaval but when the moment arrives I go off.
I have had Deja-vu many times in my past but rarely now. My dreams are usually disturbing but luckily, I do not sleep very well so they do not get chance to take hold.
I have chosen 8 poems that reflect this.

NOWHERE TO GO

I'm a creature of habits
Mostly bad
I wear the same clothing
Very sad
I eat the same breakfast
Tasteless and bland
Leave for work at the same time
Watch the big hand
But my routine this morning
Veered from the same
My automatic journey
Became a mind game
Just what if I didn't
Take the same path
Out came a nervous titter
I am not prone to laugh
A germ of an idea
Entered my head
If I went left and not right
And kept walking instead
I became edgy and sweaty
Was it something I ate
This is dangerous thinking
I must know my fate.....and NOT BE LATE!

John the poet

GETTING THERE

I went on a bicycle ride
An experience to get
Up the length of two countries
ARE WE THERE YET?

Uphill and down dale
With rain that made us wet
Then the sun came out again
ARE WE THERE YET?

Friends to keep me company
From dawn till sunset
A sandwich and pint in a pub
ARE WE THERE YET?

With my legs going round and round
And of course, a padded set!
10 miles turned into hundreds
ARE WE THERE YET?

Photo ops along the route
Blogs and phone calls let
Family and friends know where I am
ARE WE THERE YET?

Stopped when land turned into sea
Job done and this I bet
We will be doing other events like this
YES! WE ARE THERE YET?

John the poet

DEEP PHILOSOPHICAL STUFF OR TOSH?

There is talking in the streets
Thinking in the park
Questions at the supermarket
Tossing and turning in the dark

Is this revolution?
No and no again
Feel the groundswell, hear the roar
Let the tide begin

John the poet

HERE'S TO THE BAD TIMES

Those days that seemed so endless
When the world was just like Hell
You banged your head and stubbed your toe
And followed a lingering bad smell

You were skint and short of buddies
The money had run out
All seemed out to get you
There was paranoia about

Your health was like your stretched waistline
Your sex life shrunken and cold
Life, you didn't give a shag about
You felt so tired and old

So here's to the bad times
Though they are now just memory
I compare them to my recent good times
All life's circle seems to be.

John the poet

DAYBREAK

On those days when skin is thin
And the barbs of life mark and scar
The peace that is not found
In quiet moments in your car

All you seem to ache and sigh
An effort even to breathe
The knowledge of why is way too far
And miraged oases cannot be believed

....

later

On this day are futures made
Bags are packed and bills mislaid
No last look, no check, no need
The feelings already taking seed

Yesterday I did not make my stand
My life I held in my right hand
Felt the weight, the textured time
What happens now is only mine.

John the poet

NEW ENDING

New beginning, old ways
Carve a Buddha, find a cave
Wear sandals, never shave
Rules of commune
Shared air and peace
Make our clothes
Tease the fleece
Show the children
Stars and magic
Hunt for food
Death is not tragic
Life with technology
Brought the world into my space
When we could be content you see
A smaller human race
The cave has changed a bit now
Solar panels and conservatory
The hypocaust and drawing well
Updated as a progressing story
The fibre optic feed has
Replaced the rows of seeds
The satellite tracking dish
Was the wok that once cooked fish
So it's beginning with no end
A cycling time to spend
Whither holocaust or flood
Then start again for good?

John the poet

SIGNPOSTS IN MY LIFE

One step is all that's important
Out of the door, along the lane
A chance meeting, a fleeting talk
Changes direction, veers the weather vane

Do you follow Messiah like
Or store it as a wish
To hold the germ as longing
A delicacy on a dish

Now I am old I am still susceptible
To a man with a plan
An idea, a vision, an urge
To fly to foreign lands

John the poet

HERE I GO (ROOFTOP REVERIE)

I am talking to myself again
I have that look upon my place
My head thoughts spin
A coin is tossed
I am not in the human race

All my dreams of destinations
Are as clear as fog and soot
Body needs to catch up
With my mind
So an urgency takes root

At last peace and understanding
The quest seems so worthwhile
To find love and receive love
You must go the extra mile

Lincoln writers workshop homework poem

To see where you are going
You have to know where you have been
And what you have just stood in.

(A reflective moment from the Yorkshire Dales)

John the walking poet

SCOFF-ETRY

These 8 poems cover starter, main course and dessert.
I have briefly highlighted our obsession with too much, too little and even a shrinking or no food source.
Plus the ongoing imbalance of fragile supply across the globe.
So it's malnutrition versus obesity which creates different issues but similar worries
Look at the Ukrainian grain blockade and it's effect

FETCH A CLOTH

You've got dinner down your front
Gravy on your tie
Porridge in your lap
Soup is in your eye

You're a naughty boy, a bad boy
A nightmare and a mess
Run me ragged, leave me speechless
But I must confess

I see something others don't
There's potential in your head
I noticed whilst you spilled champagne
On the day that we were wed.

John the poet

WHAT WE BECAME AND ARE!

When basic need
Extends to greed
And first punch thrown
Then weapon shown
Be it food or land
We will make our stand
To protect the few
From shortage anew
Tribe and clan
Warrior man
raid and take
kill and forsake
fences built
amnesties split
borders breached
rumours to teach
strong not week
lose mild and meek
invade and burn
will we ever learn

John the poet

FOOD THAT HAS ALREADY BEEN CHEWED

Whilst grazing down the High st.
With my stomach on my mind
I had the diner's dilemma
Of what and where to find

A snack to satisfy me?
A pie to please my eye?
A Sub or Gregg with fillings?
Eat in or under sky?

Hot or cold or mixture
Freshly made last week
Check the price and taxes
Edible value is what I seek

Nothing there to entice me
Though there's lots to see
Food that looks like it's been chewed
Is unattractive to me

John the poet

CAN IT BE

I never made the boy scouts
Or owned a Swiss army pen knife
Having a simple can opener
Would have meant an easier life

I struggled at lunchtimes
Accessing soups and stew
And often would go hungry
With clearing up to do

The task in store was easy
The chain saw was impressive
But now see the far-flung contents
I realise now it was excessive

So practicality is paramount
Keep utensils in your pocket
Not explosives to crack the can
Or dinner will leave you like a rocket

John the poet

BRAN CHANGES EVERYTHING

(READ/SANG TO THE RHYTHM/TUNE OF" LOVE CHANGES EVERYTHING")

Look into the fridge tonight
Feeling bloated, stomach pain
Nothing there to delight
All my cravings don't remain

(chorus)Yes bran it changes everything
It's natures friend and makes you go
So keep the toilet door in sight
For when you need to, you will know

What I need now is a movement
Some activity down below
So out comes the fruit and fibre
And reactions do soon show
(repeat chorus)

So I'm sitting in the I office now
An appointment with Mr Brown
Could be in there for quite a while
Newspaper open, trouser down
(repeat chorus)

John the poet

BELLY ACHE

In all the bellies of the world
Is there food or space
Does the ache that dwells there
Reflect onto their face

Is it hunger or indigestion
Gluttony or a drought
Go on a diet, chew a root
To feed or go without

The swollen stomachs show
That we are maybe all the same
Eat too much, no food to touch
So abstain and look to blame

John the poet

THE SQUEAKY WALLED CAFE

I was feeling very peckish
In a shrunken belly style
Breakfast has evaded me
And I had to walk a mile

The A board advert caught my eye
A frying smell caught my nose
A jumbo bacon butty called
I'll have one of those

On entering the establishment
With hunger on my mind
Alarm bellies started to sound
As what I was to find

The chip pan was from antiques roadshow
Using original fat
Two unhealthy looking diners
Shovelling full breakfasts where they sat

The butty arrived eventually
It wasn't even meat
The grease was running out the bag
I was running down the street

The moral of this butty
Is true as it was real
Put your mistake in the litterbin
And let it quickly congeal

John the poet

I AM UNSURE ABOUT MY BODY

I am unsure about my body
I seem fat but often thin.
Being conscious of the latest vogue
I could be out or even in.

This week's diet in the fridge
Is more beneficial than the last five.
I have cut out red-label foods
To make me so alive.

But I need a pill for my lethargy
To supplement my lack of strength.
To reach that toned Nirvana
I will go to any length.

I admit I have been under the knife
And fork and spoon as well
A binge diet is what I need
Then a counsellor to tell.

I am exploring facial surgery
To compliment my lithesome grace
But I can only afford one eyebrow.
So here's my new tattooed face

John the poet

Backword

A Backword can be an ending or could be a bridge
to another Foreword.
They could in fact be a tipping point and I have
had my points tipped many times.
I can usually finish up on a ledge but it needs an
upgraded device to get me in the fog of confusion.
Since I entered the technological age (shortly after
the Jurassic) I have tried to hold on to an OS that I
have just worked out but that falls over with lots of
error messages and so I have had to reinvest and
venture into the new void.
Going to cloud (one drive) storage sent my files
into a secret locker in a hidden room.
Is all my best work floating about somewhere. Is
Indiana Jones free?
Or is it already published in Manic Reflections, or
Deflections or Inspections
You choose.

John the poet signing off

Thankyou for reading my work
John